DIGGING UP
the Past

Emperor Qin's Terra-Cotta Army

Essential Library

An Imprint of Abdo Publishing | www.abdopublishing.com

DIGGING UP
the Past

Emperor Qin's Terra-Cotta Army

BY DIANE BAILEY

CONTENT CONSULTANT
JOHN KONG-CHEONG LEUNG
ASSOCIATE PROFESSOR OF ASIAN HISTORY
NORTHERN ARIZONA UNIVERSITY

www.abdopublishing.com

Published by Abdo Publishing, a division of ABDO, PO Box 398166, Minneapolis, Minnesota 55439. Copyright © 2015 by Abdo Consulting Group, Inc. International copyrights reserved in all countries. No part of this book may be reproduced in any form without written permission from the publisher. Essential Library™ is a trademark and logo of Abdo Publishing.

Printed in the United States of America, North Mankato, Minnesota
032014
092014

THIS BOOK CONTAINS
RECYCLED MATERIALS

Cover Photo: iStockphoto/Thinkstock
Interior Photos: iStockphoto/Thinkstock, 2, 9; Neal Ulevich/AP Images, 6; Volina/Shutterstock Images, 9 (inset); Nat Krause, 11; Hung Chung Chih/Shutterstock Images, 13, 54, 66; Martin Schutt/picture-alliance/dpa/AP Images, 17; SuperStock/Glow Images, 18; AP Images, 20, 22, 23; Raymond Darolle/Sygma/Corbis, 27, 90; Yuan Jingzhi/Imaginechina/AP Images, 29, 60; Zang Jin/Imaginechina/AP Images, 30; Fine Art Images/Heritage Images/Glow Images, 34; Keren Su/Corbis, 36; Hsein-Min Yang/National Geographic/Getty Images, 40; Jason Lewis/DK Images, 43; T. J. Kirkpatrick/Corbis, 46; Aldo Pavan/Grand Tour/Corbis, 49; Xu Xiaolin/Corbis, 51, 75; Imaginechina/AP Images, 53; Shutterstock Images, 57; O. Louis Mazzatenta/National Geographic Society/Corbis, 65; Richard Drew/AP Images, 71; Harley Couper/Shutterstock Images, 77; Bettmann/Corbis, 78; JTB Photo/Glow Images, 82; Ruan Banhui/Imaginechina/AP Images, 86; Tim Graham/Robert Harding/Glow Images, 88; Public Domain, 94; Lukas Hlavac/Shutterstock Images, 97

Editor: Arnold Ringstad
Series Designer: Becky Daum

Library of Congress Control Number: 2014932246

Cataloging-in-Publication Data

Bailey, Diane.
 Emperor Qin's Terra-cotta Army / Diane Bailey.
  p. cm. -- (Digging up the past)
Includes bibliographical references and index.
ISBN 978-1-62403-232-5
1. Qin shi huang, Emperor of China, 259-210 B.C.--Tomb--Juvenile literature.   2. Terra-cotta sculpture, Chinese--Qin-Han dynasties, 221 B.C.-220 A.D.--Juvenile literature.   3. Shaanxi Sheng (China)--Antiquities--Juvenile literature. I. Title.
931/.04--dc23
                                        2014932246

CONTENTS

1

A Silent Army

One March day in 1974, with the imposing Mount Li rising behind them, the Yang brothers discussed a problem they faced. The farmers lived in Shaanxi Province in central China, near the city of Xi'an. Their trouble was something farmers have struggled with since people first began growing food: they needed water for their crops.

The Yang brothers had no idea that a world of priceless artifacts was buried underneath their farm.

In an ordinary year, rain would wash down the sides of Mount Li, but that year, the weather had been too dry. With no end to the drought in sight, the Yang brothers needed another solution. If water would not come to them, they would have to go and find some.

DIGGING DOWN

They chose a spot and began to dig a wide, deep well. Before long, their shovels hit something hard in the dry, packed earth. Shards of broken pottery began surfacing as the brothers continued digging. Then they hit something else. This time, it was not a pot. It was the torso of a body. The brothers quickly realized they had found not the corpse of a real person, but a statue made from terra-cotta.

The brothers were not surprised to find the bits of pottery. For decades, people had found the remains of kilns and artifacts left behind by the people of ancient China. The country was rich in history—there was always a little bit of it underfoot. A clay person, on the other hand, was much more interesting. However, it also made the brothers uncomfortable. They began to suspect they had stumbled upon a temple rather than a kiln. Such a discovery might attract the attention of the authorities.

The Yang brothers did not want any trouble. But they still needed water, so they kept digging. More of this clay man began to appear, including his head, arms, and legs. The statue was broken, but the pieces were there. And it was not just the man himself. The brothers unearthed other objects, too. Sharp bronze arrowheads were embedded in the earth next to the body, along with several bronze pieces later identified as the trigger pieces for ancient crossbows.

WHERE IS THE TERRA-COTTA ARMY?

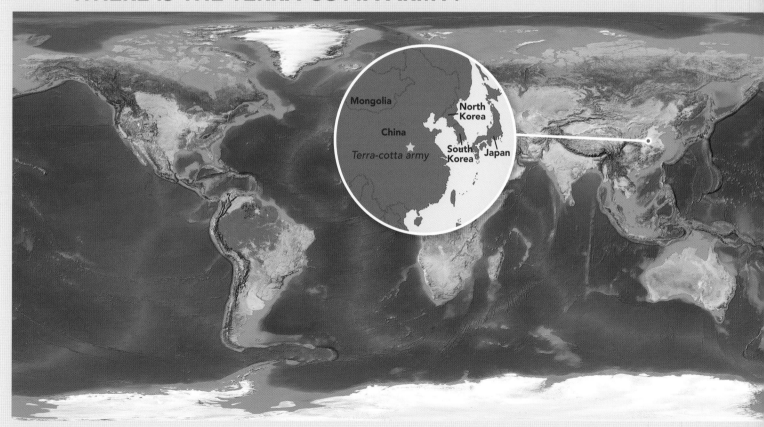

QIN

The word *Qin* sounds like "chin" and is sometimes written that way: Ch'in. Some language experts believe the modern English name *China* comes from these roots. The power of the Qin state and the fact that the country was united under Qin rule suggest this is a logical conclusion to explain the word's etymology. However, the ancient language Sanskrit seems to have embraced the related words *sin* and *cin* centuries before the first emperor took over, suggesting the name may have stemmed from a different region altogether.

The clay man was in poor condition, his battered torso having been trapped in the ground for centuries. He did not look like much to the untrained eye. But the Yang brothers—and the whole world—soon discovered he was an astonishing glimpse into the 2,000-year-old world of ancient China.

THE UNDERGROUND WARRIORS

It turned out the clay man was a soldier. Even more significantly, it turned out he was not alone. He was just one of thousands in a huge terra-cotta army. Once they began digging, archaeologists realized they had stumbled onto one of the largest finds in history. Since that first discovery, archaeologists have uncovered more than 2,000 soldiers in a series of three underground pits, and they are not anywhere close to being finished. Experts estimate there are probably 7,000 to 8,000 soldiers altogether.[1]

All of these soldiers were gathered together for one purpose: to guard the tomb of Qin Shihuangdi, the first emperor of China, and protect him in the afterlife. As the dig continued, archaeologists discovered the terra-cotta troops stood watch over a whole underground city constructed to become Qin's home for eternity.

Qin is an important figure in Chinese history. He unified the country approximately 2,200 years ago, a feat that is still considered among the most important events in the nation's history. By most accounts, the emperor was a ruler who did not hesitate to exercise his power to get what he wanted. He desired a tomb more lavish than anything ever constructed before, and once he was in power, he ordered his subjects to work on the project.

A modern statue of Qin now stands near the terra-cotta army site.

DIGGING
DEEPER

Identity Crisis

Chinese professor Liu Jiusheng has suggested an intriguing alternative theory about the terra-cotta figures' role in Qin's life. While most historians believe they are soldiers, Liu says they are not. He argues common soldiers would not have been permitted to be so close to the emperor. Instead, he thinks they are servants and bodyguards inspired by officials in Qin's court, a royal entourage for the emperor's afterlife. Liu supports his theory by pointing out the soldiers are significantly taller than an average Chinese man. Some art scholars attribute the figures' greater height to the Chinese tradition of sculpting figures slightly larger than life to make them imposing. Liu says their size indicates they ranked high in the social hierarchy.

Another Chinese historian, Chen Jingyuan, argues the figures do belong to an army, but not to Qin's. Chen thinks the army was constructed a century earlier for Empress Xuan, who died more than 50 years before Qin was born. She was a powerful woman who had the financial means to order such a project. Chen points out that the warriors are located as far as 0.9 miles (1.4 km) from the rest of Qin's mausoleum. Chen finds it strange that, if the funeral figures did belong to Qin, they are situated so far away. In addition, he says the warriors' clothing and hair are characteristic of styles common to the ethnicity of the empress, rather than of Qin.

The identity of the terra-cotta figures has been called into question by some scholars.

The amount of labor that went into the project was staggering. To excavate the trenches where the army would stand guard, workers dug up 130,000 cubic yards (99,000 cu m) of earth without the help of heavy machinery. They used 10,500 cubic yards (8,000 cu m) of wood to build the roofs of the pits. To pave the floors, they used 250,000 bricks.[2] The three pits of soldiers are only one area on the outskirts of Qin's underground city. Archaeologists have identified hundreds of pits, containing some 50,000 figures, weapons, and artifacts.[3] They all surround the crown jewel, the burial mound of Qin himself. It is the largest tomb in the world, with the complex sprawling over some 22 square miles (57 sq km).[4] Scholars frequently use the term *mausoleum* to describe the tomb complex, though it is not a mausoleum in the traditional sense—an aboveground tomb. The tomb itself still lies entirely belowground. It has never been directly excavated.

Shortly after the first warriors were discovered, construction began to turn the site into a huge museum. It has become a popular tourist site that welcomes some 5 million visitors each

> **"There are seven wonders in the world, and we may say that the discovery of these terra-cotta warriors and horses is the eighth."[5]**
>
> —JACQUES CHIRAC, FORMER PRESIDENT OF FRANCE AND CHINESE HISTORY ENTHUSIAST

year. In 1987, it was selected as a World Heritage Site by the United Nations Educational, Scientific and Cultural Organization (UNESCO).

INTO THE SPIRIT WORLD

In ancient times, people in China and elsewhere believed the dead would pass into another kind of life. Their mortal bodies were gone, but their souls would survive and continue to live as their earthly ones did. In order to prepare for this next life, important people were often buried with the things they had customarily used during their lives on Earth. These things ranged from the useful and practical, such as clothing or dishes, to the decorative and entertaining, such as musical instruments or jewelry. Some of the objects were real; others, such as the terra-cotta soldiers, represented their living counterparts. The more important a person was, the more went into his or her tomb—and no one was more important than Qin.

Animals and even people were often buried with the dead. Sometimes these people were killed before

QIN AND GEOMANCY

Geomancy is an ancient Chinese practice that dictates the placement of buildings and objects with the goal of creating harmony. According to this belief, the way things are arranged and the directions they face could have lasting consequences to the people who live there. In keeping with this system, Qin's tomb is located in a hill and is protected by nearby rivers that form boundaries. The emperor's underground armies are located to the east of his tomb, the most likely direction from which afterlife enemies would have invaded.

15

being buried. Other times they were buried alive. By the time of Qin's death, the practice of burying people alongside wealthy citizens had long since fallen out of favor. Writers from as long ago as the 500s BCE commented on the practice only in the past tense. It would have been especially impractical to sacrifice an entire living army that was needed to fight real wars in real life. However, there was a loophole that still allowed for Qin's protection in the afterlife. The ancient Chinese also believed statues of people could do this job. In the eyes of Qin and his craftsmen, being buried with clay figures was just as good as having the real thing.

GUARDING THE PAST

The finds at Qin's mausoleum attest to the emperor's power and his desire for everlasting life. But they also tell the collective life story of the millions of ordinary Chinese people who lived under his rule.

Lined up in their underground trenches, awaiting their call to duty, the terra-cotta soldiers are a work of

Seeing the army in person continues to ignite the imagination of visitors from the local area and across the world.

art on the grandest scale. But even more amazing is that their builders never intended for them to be seen by human eyes. They were meant to remain buried for eternity alongside their emperor. Instead, today their faces spur the imaginations of archaeologists, scholars, and everyday visitors.

With steady hands and precision tools, archaeologists have spent decades tenderly brushing away the dirt of the past and preserving the warriors to present them to new generations. Aided by modern scientific techniques, scholars are working to tell the soldiers' stories. Fortunately, for a silent army, they have much to say.

The Discovery

Finding the terra-cotta soldiers was not a complete surprise for some. Stories had circulated among the people who lived in the area, and people always knew something was buried under their feet. Over the years, peasants had stumbled on odd finds, including pieces of pottery and even the occasional head or body of a buried statue. In 1948, a farmer unearthed a terra-cotta statue of a kneeling servant. A second one emerged in 1956. Altogether, between

Only a few decades after the discovery, the farms around the site were replaced by a large museum complex.

1932 and 1970, there were records of five kneeling servants found in the area.[1]

However, people were conscious of respecting the dead. When they did find artifacts, they often reburied them to keep them hidden or simply destroyed them. The finds might cause a flurry of whispers and rumors among the villagers, but they were not always reported as important historical discoveries.

Few people could have imagined the sheer scope of what lay beneath them. Historical documents reported the emperor's tomb was encased in Mount Li, but there was no easy way to get in and no real reason to try. Villagers might have wondered or dreamed, but they had more pressing concerns than a bunch of cracked and faded shards of sculpture or pottery. There was no practical use for a broken pot, after all. People in rural China were poor, and they kept busy just trying to scrape out a living.

Still, word got around in the spring of 1974, and neighbors came to see what the Yang brothers had found. Some remarked the relics looked like statues of ancient Chinese gods. Other visitors just came to see if they could

During the time of the army's discovery, most Chinese people lived rural lives.

get anything of value. A few enterprising people collected the first bronze arrowheads found at the site and took them to a recycling center where they could be sold as scrap metal. Villagers and onlookers were partly worried about the discovery and partly intrigued. Mostly, they were unsure of how best to proceed.

POLITICS

One potential problem with reporting the find had to do with the political climate of China during the mid-1970s. In 1949, Communist leader Mao Zedong had taken over the government of China, and he was still in power 25 years later. Mao was an authoritarian ruler who pushed through many drastic industrial and agricultural reforms and reorganizations in the late 1950s. The changes served Mao's political purposes but brought about devastating economic consequences under which many Chinese people suffered terribly. Protesting was dangerous. Mao often punished people who spoke out against his policies.

In 1966, splits between factions in China's Communist government led to the Cultural Revolution. During this time, political, social, economic and even cultural issues deeply divided China's society. A radical mass movement launched by Mao and others swept across the face of the country. The changes threw thousands of institutions

Participants in the Cultural Revolution held up copies of Mao's writings and portraits of Communist thinker Karl Marx.

QIN BRICKS

Brick making thrived during Qin's rule. Sturdy but decorative bricks were used to build walls and floors of buildings, and as the kingdom expanded, production of these bricks increased. Bricks from this era became highly prized artifacts to collectors. They were believed to bring good luck, and wealthy people eagerly sought them out for use as pillows. Though they were not the most comfortable headrests, people believed the power within the brick improved their physical well-being. The supposed benefits included making them calmer, helping them see better, and allowing them to live longer.

and millions of people into fateful, and often fatal, turmoil. The teaching of history became one of the most contentious cultural issues during the Cultural Revolution. China's history stretched back thousands of years, but Mao forbade the celebration of much of this history. The Cultural Revolution continued into the 1970s, when the first traces of the terra-cotta army were discovered.

However, even during the Cultural Revolution, Mao's Communist government officially encouraged archaeology. The idea was to promote the worth of common people over that of an imperial ruler. Precious artifacts were physical proof to remind citizens of the extravagance of past emperors while at the same time celebrating the ordinary Chinese citizens who had made the artifacts in the first place.

Shortly after the Yang brothers' discovery, local official Fang Shumin came to see what was going on. Along with the weapons, the brothers had also found bricks. Originally, these bricks were dark blue and decorated with detailed designs. Now they were old and worn down. Still, even in their aged condition, Fang recognized the bricks: they dated to the time of Qin.

GAINING ATTENTION

About a month after the initial discovery, Fang reported the find to local museum curator Zhao Kangmin. Intrigued, Zhao rode his bicycle to the site to take a look. Immediately, he understood the potential significance of the discovery. He examined the few pieces already unearthed and recognized they dated to the Qin dynasty. If the pieces had something to do with the first emperor, it could shed new light on China's history. Zhao took some fragments home and began restoring them. Two months later, he finished reconstructing two warriors from the pieces unearthed at the site.

Like the villagers, Zhao was nervous about reporting the find to the Chinese government. As a historian, he studied China's ancient emperors and the social and political system of feudalism that had dominated China for centuries. However, feudalism

FEUDALISM IN CHINA

Feudalism took hold in China during the Zhou dynasty, which lasted from approximately 1046 to 256 BCE. Under this social structure, peasants worked on land belonging to their lords. They provided labor and loyalty. In return the lords protected the peasants, gave them a place to live, and provided enough food to survive. In a feudal society, lords were bound to provide some services to the country's ruler, but they still possessed a great deal of local power.

was contradictory to China's political system in the 1970s. Communist China promoted a unified nation run by a central government. Feudalism relied, at least in part, on family ties and favoritism. Even showing an interest in it was considered suspicious. Several years before, Zhao had run afoul of the authorities. Because of his interests, they accused him of encouraging feudalism.

By luck, a news reporter visiting his family in the area heard about the discovery and wrote a short article about it. His story caught the attention of government officials, who sent a team of archaeologists

THE RIGHT TOOLS

At a huge archaeological site, figuring out exactly where to dig can be a daunting task. Archaeologists have a tool that can help. The Luoyang shovel, developed in China, has a long, narrow blade that allows it to be inserted easily into the ground and then pulled back holding a small sample of earth.

The digger can then assess the character of the dirt to determine if it is compacted, loose, pure, or mixed with other material. This information gives experts information on whether structures or artifacts are likely to be buried there and provides guidance on whether to keep digging.

Much of the early preservation work took place entirely at the site of the tomb.

to investigate. It may have helped that Mao was an admirer of Qin. Mao famously said, "Let the past serve the present."[2] He praised the ancient emperor's style of using past events to fuel changes in the present, rather than as examples of how to preserve the status quo. An excavation of Qin's tomb would, of course, be a look into the past. However, in this case it could reinforce Mao's leadership style.

Four months after the first relics of the terra-cotta army were discovered, the Chinese government began excavating the site in earnest. It quickly expanded beyond the confines of the Yang brothers' farm. In a 2009 interview, archaeologist Yuan Zhongyi remembered the site's expansion: "First, we excavated around the area the farmers drilled and found the relic site to be much, much larger than expected. It took us about half a year to find the edge of the site."[3] Today, the mausoleum complex is enormous, containing thousands of clay warriors as well as other artifacts. Uncovering all of that takes time, and the dig continues to this day. Each new discovery within Qin's lavish mausoleum offers more proof the emperor was determined to have every earthly comfort, even in the afterlife. It is a testament to his power and a window on how he used that power to transform the nation of China.

YUAN ZHONGYI

Yuan Zhongyi was one of the first archaeologists to begin studying the terra-cotta warriors, and he has become a renowned expert on the topic. In college, Yuan studied the history of ancient China. After graduating in 1963, he became involved with research in the Xi'an region of China. He was a natural choice to lead the archaeological team charged with excavating Qin's warriors.

Yuan first arrived at the site in July 1974. He spent the next 30 years working with the terra-cotta army, including a ten-year period from 1988 to 1998 as the director for the site's museum. Even after retiring, Yuan served as a consultant to the excavations. In 2009, he remarked, "I've spent most of my life digging. Archaeological excavation is boring work, but I often feel a happiness that outsiders won't be able to understand because it is heaven for archaeologists."[4]

Yuan's museum is now among the most popular tourist sites in all of China.

3

The First Emperor

When he was born into the royal family of the Kingdom of Qin in 259 BCE, China's future first emperor was named Ying Zheng. His father died in 246 and Zheng succeeded him, becoming king of the Qin state at the age of 13. He was too young to run the empire alone just yet, but already he was good at looking out for himself. He lived a luxurious lifestyle, and he wanted one even after he died. To ensure this, Zheng embarked on a mausoleum

The largely earthen Great Wall constructed by Qin was later built over with sturdier stone sections.

project, ordering his subjects to begin constructing an afterlife city for him to live in.

He was busy extending his earthly power, as well. When Zheng became king, China was in the midst of turmoil and change. During the Warring States period between 475 and 221, seven independent states—Qin, Han, Zhao, Wei, Yan, Chu, and Qi—vied for control and supremacy. Fighting spread across China, and the demand for soldiers was constant. Rather than just sending nobility into battle, as had been the past custom, the constant wars opened the door for commoners to join the military and advance in status by proving their worth on the battlefield. The Qin

ONE HUNDRED SCHOOLS OF THOUGHT

From the 700s BCE into the Warring States period, China underwent profound growth in its economy, technology, and social development. Centralized, bureaucratic forms of government began to take hold as China's states sought to conquer one another, and commoners gained new power through the expanded military. The tension between the classes led to philosophical clashes. Many different ideological approaches formed to help make sense of the changing social climate. Confucianism, Taoism, and Qin's legalism were just some of the major players in what came to be known as the One Hundred Schools of Thought.

state steadily gained power thanks to its fearsome soldiers. One historian noted, "The infantry and cavalry of [Qin] were great in number. The foot soldiers wore no helmets and engaged the enemy with untold ferocity. The mounts of the cavalry were so swift that they could jump twelve paces."[1]

Zheng was determined to conquer all the lands of China and unite them under his rule. Advisers assisted him during the early years of his reign, but he took over sole command in 238 at the age of 22. Over the next 17 years he systematically vanquished his enemies, bringing the other Chinese states under Qin rule. Ancient historian Sima Qian, who wrote *Records of the Grand Historian* in 109 BCE, noted the king worked through his rivals "like a silkworm devouring a mulberry leaf."[2] By 221, Zheng had achieved his goal. China was a unified nation.

With his power consolidated, Zheng decided to publicize his victory and cement his control. Merely being king seemed insufficient. According to ancient historian Sima Qian, Zheng said, "Now if some change in title is not carried out, there will be no way to celebrate these achievements and make them known to later generations. Let deliberations be held on an imperial title."[3] Zheng's new title became Qin Shihuangdi. *Qin* referred to the nation; *shi* is the Chinese word for "first," and *huangdi* combined two words meaning "imperial" and "ruler." The result was a new position: emperor. It was the first time in Chinese history such a title had been used.

TAKING CONTROL

With all of China now under his direct rule, Qin began modernizing the state. He was a hands-on ruler, paying close attention to day-to-day business around his empire. Qin's first order of business was to abolish the old feudal system. He instituted a hierarchical government, with centralized offices overseeing smaller, local authorities. This structure was ideal for the wide-ranging changes he began implementing throughout the country.

One of his most important accomplishments was standardizing the system of writing. When China was divided, each state used its own system of characters to represent

As emperor, Qin set out to create an efficient, ruthless empire.

words or ideas. Qin replaced it with what is now known as small seal script. The number of characters was reduced, simplifying the language. The new system was formally designated as the language for all of China. Qin also helped promote the economy and trade by standardizing systems of money and measurements. For example, he ordered that the width of the wheel ruts in roads be the same throughout the land, allowing carriages to travel easily across the large nation.

The Great Wall of China was among Qin's largest projects. Though the effort largely involved connecting an existing series of small walls, it was still an amazing feat of construction. Some 1,500 miles (2,400 km) long, the wall protected Qin's empire from warring nomadic tribes in the north.[4]

The wall also illustrated Qin's rigid approach to power. Hundreds of thousands of unpaid workers worked on the wall. Many of Qin's projects helped China and continue to influence it today. But his style of rule often came at the expense of the Chinese people.

TOURING THE EMPIRE

Qin traveled frequently through his empire, undertaking inspections of his subjects. While traveling, he ordered stone or wooden plaques be inscribed with his accomplishments and installed throughout the countryside. These served as reminders of the changes he had brought and reinforced the notion he was the nation's supreme ruler. One read, "The universe entire is our emperor's realm. . . . Wherever human life is found, all acknowledge his sovereignty."[5]

PHILOSOPHY

Although he was not a scholar, Qin did have intellectual leanings. He subscribed to the views of Han Fei, a scholar who supported the policies of an earlier Chinese statesman, Shang Yang. Both men believed rulers could not afford to be too benevolent, or else their authority would be ignored. They also thought people were primarily motivated by fear and greed, and they felt strict laws were necessary to keep the citizenry in line. Under this philosophy, called legalism, the law applied to everyone equally, with one big exception: a ruler could never be considered equal to his subjects. Legalism fit Qin's approach to ruling. He had big plans and no patience for naysayers.

Qin sought counsel from Li Si, a scholar who joined his administration shortly after he became king. A believer in legalism, Li became the emperor's trusted adviser. It was Li Si who recommended Qin promote his own philosophy by destroying evidence of any other ways of thinking. Books reflecting alternative schools of thought were ordered burned, although practical books about medicine or agriculture were spared. Scholars and other people who disobeyed the order were executed. Li Si commented, "As for persons who wish to study, let them take the officials as their teachers."[6]

Qin remains an important figure in Chinese history today and has been memorialized in statue form.

PREDICTION FROM THE SKY

One story holds that in 211 BCE, a meteorite was found with an inscription claiming the nation would be divided after Qin's death. Furious and unnerved, Qin ordered an investigation to discover who had dared to create such an inscription. Not surprisingly, no one confessed. As punishment, Qin ordered everyone living in the village where it was found killed. The stone itself was burned and then pulverized into dust. Qin's efforts to erase this prophecy were in vain, however—he died the next year.

SEARCHING FOR ETERNAL LIFE

Qin was efficient, but his domineering style earned him few real friends. As he gained more power, he also became more paranoid about his future—or lack thereof. Qin believed only one fate was truly fitting for the first emperor of China: immortality. Even for someone as powerful as an emperor, that was a tall order, but Qin was determined to try. He assigned alchemists, magicians, and astrologers to the project of keeping him alive forever, ordering them to find a magic elixir that would do the trick. He traveled across China on this quest but always came up empty-handed.

It was a race against time, and eventually death won. During a tour of his empire, Qin suddenly became ill and died in 210. Before his death, he wrote a letter naming his oldest son as his heir. But after the emperor died, one of his advisers, Zhao Gao, hatched a plot to take power. First, Zhao covered up the news of Qin's death from all but a close circle of people. When the emperor's entourage returned to the city,

Zhao arranged for a carriage of salted fish to travel behind the carriage containing the emperor's body to disguise the smell of his decaying corpse. For two months, Zhao pretended to be conversing behind closed doors with the emperor. Instead he was setting his plan into action. He convinced Qin's oldest son, the rightful heir, that his father had not named him to the throne. Instead, Zhao managed to install one of Qin's younger sons, who was weaker and more susceptible to manipulation.

The plan worked, but only for a few years. Qin's merciless rule had created unrest among the peasantry, and a series of rebellions occurred. Only five years after Qin's death, the last of his heirs was ousted. The Qin dynasty, which the emperor had expected to last thousands of generations, had ended after only 15 years. Yet the changes he had brought to China were designed to make the country strong and lasting, and in that he was successful. The technological, social, and political advancements that began under Qin would transform China into a powerful nation that would profoundly influence the development of civilization.

4

Glimpses into the Past

The discovery of one soldier led to an army. A handful of pits led to dozens more. For decades, the treasures at Qin's mausoleum complex have continued to surface. After the first warriors were found in the 1970s, archaeologists went on to find bronze replicas of his personal chariots in 1980, a pit full of stone armor in 1998, and several pits with models of performers, civil servants, and animals in the 1990s and 2000s. The existence of another underground room in Qin's tomb was reported

As more and more pits and chambers were discovered, archaeologists began to understand the scale of Qin's enormous construction effort.

BUILDING WITH DIRT

Dirt is strong, durable, cheap, and widely available. It was one of the preferred building materials for Qin's workers. First, workers combined a moist mixture of sand, clay, and gravel. Then they poured it into a wooden frame, pounded it down until it was dense and hard, let it dry, and removed the frame. Many roads traversing the Qin kingdom were made using this rammed earth technique. The builders of his mausoleum also used it to construct the underground walls of the pits.

in 2007, and 2012 brought news of more than 100 additional soldiers. Each new discovery has helped fill in the blanks of Qin's intriguing story—including how he managed to execute such an enormous project.

Building a city from scratch was the task Qin set before his people. The project was so big that after nearly four decades, workers still had not finished when the emperor died. But thanks to his strict style of rule, with little tolerance for failure, they had made a lot of progress.

The logistics of such an effort were daunting, and the first hurdle was staffing. Ancient historian Sima Qian recorded that building Qin's mausoleum required 700,000 workers.[1] However, historians have called this number into question, pointing out such a workforce would have been larger than the population of any city at the time. Assembling all those people, finding them places to live, and feeding them would have posed huge challenges. It may have required far fewer people, especially since there are indications the process was highly organized and represented an early

Thanks to his regime's efficiency, Qin may have used a relatively small workforce to construct the warriors and their complex.

example of assembly-line production.

Under Qin's bureaucratic government, administrators assigned specific duties to each person for maximum efficiency. Etched on the hips or under the arms of the statues, investigations have found the names of dozens of master craftsmen who led the project of sculpting the warriors. Each of these

master artisans had many apprentices, bringing the total number of statue builders to approximately 1,530.[2]

Some of the workers were professionals, but many were just regular people drafted into the enormous undertaking. Regardless of a worker's experience or expertise, Qin would not tolerate shoddy production. As a form of quality control, each statue was required to be signed with the name of the person who made it. Upon inspection, if something was not up to the standard, the worker would be punished. The same principle applied to the manufacture of weapons.

QIN'S WORKERS

Researchers have wondered about the origins of the tomb workers. A common theory suggests they hailed from China's northern regions. But there are other possibilities. Skeletons of 121 workers—all male, with an average age of 24—were found in a mass grave near the tomb. DNA testing indicated that one of them came from western Eurasia, in the modern-day region of India, Pakistan, and Iran. He may have been a prisoner of war or a trader who decided to move to a new place. Additional evidence on the origins of workers could shed new light on how the workforce was assembled, as well as on how people moved around in the Qin era.

A GROWING ARMY

Forming the backbone of Qin's army are his thousands of soldiers, which are carefully arranged in battle formation and illustrate the nature of war in Qin times. Pit One, the largest of three main pits, measures more than 17,000 square yards (14,000 sq m)—almost as large as three football fields.[3] Qin's main army, composed mostly of infantry, stands at the ready in this pit. The majority of the warriors have not yet been excavated, but archaeologists estimate the pit holds approximately 6,000 statues in total. Most of them are lined up in long, parallel columns—a standby formation as they await their call to duty. At the front are three rows of archers, a vanguard to initiate the attack on the enemy. One row would shoot while the others reloaded. In between the bowmen and the infantry are the war chariots, each manned by a charioteer. One or two soldiers stood beside each chariot. Armed with 20-foot (6 m) lances, they could keep a sufficient distance from the enemy to prevent their horses from being injured.[4]

In 1976, archaeologists found two more large pits. Pit Two is approximately 7,175 square yards (6,000 sq m) in size and contains a wider variety of figures, including infantry, cavalrymen, and horses. The arrangements of the soldiers show the Qin military used a variety of formations to fit battle conditions, with the core army in Pit One providing

a solid wall of human power and the additional specialized units in Pit Two providing flexibility for unusual conditions.

Pit Three, at approximately 622 square yards (520 sq m), is the smallest of the three main pits. Designed in a U shape, its contents suggest it is the army headquarters. There are 68 men, including officers, and a command chariot. Animal remains indicate ritual sacrifices were performed here prior to battle, perhaps to predict the outcome.

A fourth pit was also discovered, but it was empty. Scholars are not sure why, but one theory is that Qin's workers ran out of time and left it unfinished when Qin died. It might also have been deliberately unused because it symbolized the battlefield.

LOOTING AND DESTRUCTION

Although the mausoleum was designed to protect Qin from his enemies in the afterlife, it was vulnerable to his living enemies. In the years following his death, political tumult led to rebellions, and power changed hands several times before the more stable Han dynasty took control in 206 BCE.

Pit Two is smaller than Pit One, yet it still contains approximately 1,000 soldiers, 400 horses, and 89 chariots.

DIGGING DEEPER

The Bronze Chariots

In 1980, in a trench approximately 20 yards (18 m) east of Qin's tomb, archaeologists found thousands of bronze fragments—the pieces of two bronze chariots and horses.[5] At roughly half of life size, they are exquisite replicas of the emperor's personal transportation system. Each is manned by a charioteer and pulled by four horses. The first chariot, called High Chariot, was equipped with bronze bows and arrows and served as an advance guard to the second, called Comfortable Chariot. It is constructed like a small, squat house. Enclosed and roofed, with cushioned seats, it has detailed blinds allowing the emperor to look out, but not be seen by those outside. The chariots are painted, with the walls covered in pictures of clouds populated by immortals. Five colors are used: red, black, blue, yellow, and white.

The horses' harnesses are crafted from gold and silver. The thin bronze wires holding them together are themselves astonishing proof of how seriously the sculptors took their job. The different metals in the alloy were carefully selected so each individual part has a strength matching the amount of weight it had to support.

Some of Qin's chariots are now housed within a nearby museum rather than being left in the pits.

During this upheaval, enemies of the Qin dynasty raided the emperor's underground tomb. They might have wanted to destroy it simply to erase the memory of Qin and his power. Alternately, they may have had a more practical motivation. While the terra-cotta soldiers were not real, their weapons were. A rebel army would have needed anything they could get their hands on. Some evidence suggests looters entered the underground pits not to smash things but to steal them.

Remains of charred wood suggest a devastating fire spread through Pit One. Scholars do not know how it started. Perhaps it was the looters, leaving a final message once they were finished taking what they wanted. Or maybe

A STOLEN HEAD

Qin's ancient enemies stole the clay soldiers' weapons, but more modern thieves have recognized the value in the soldiers themselves. In 1985, a young, unemployed Chinese man came up with a get-rich-quick scheme. The terra-cotta warriors were well-known throughout China, but security at the museum was lax. Wang Yengdi, assisted by a friend who worked at the museum, stole a terra-cotta head one night after the museum closed. He believed it could later be sold for huge sums of money on the black market. Wang was caught, however, and executed for his crime.

it was an accident caused by the errant flame of a torch. Either way, it caused enormous damage. The clay soldiers and their bronze weapons did not burn, but the wood supporting the walls and ceiling did. The roof collapsed, crushing the army below.

PAINSTAKING WORK

To date, archaeologists have not found a single one of Qin's clay warriors completely intact. Instead, each figure is in pieces,

Reassembling the smashed remains of the terra-cotta warriors is a slow process.

sometimes as many as 200 of them.[6] Qin employed thousands of workers to build his underground city, and today a modern army of archaeologists is putting it back together. Teams of workers study the statues, draw and photograph them, and determine which pieces go where. It is slow work. It takes approximately three months to put a warrior back together. Song Yun, an archaeologist who worked on the soldiers for decades, said, "If we find one piece that fits in one day, that's a lucky day."[7]

Fitting the pieces together involves intense trial and error. Once something has been broken, however, nothing will restore it completely to its original state. The warriors all have small missing or mismatched parts. Archaeologists cannot always find or repair everything. However, they can often fill in gaps by taking clues from the surrounding warriors.

When restorers find pieces that fit, they use plaster to temporarily hold them together while they look for other pieces. They avoid using strong adhesives at this early stage, just in case the pieces do not actually go together. When it comes time to apply the final glue, they only have approximately 24 hours to put

IMPERFECTIONS

In recent years, restorers have not tried to repair the warriors as meticulously as they possibly could. Instead, they have left in some of the imperfections. In many places, wear on the pieces means they no longer fit together perfectly. Rather than try to fill in gaps or hide them, the restorers deliberately leave them for visitors to see.

Piecing together the
warriors requires
extreme patience and
delicacy.

together a statue before the
glue dries. Each finished warrior
provides more details about this
ancient army.

Piecing together the warriors requires extreme patience and delicacy.

5

The Figures in the Pits

The sea of faces rising from the corridors of the warriors' trenches is imposing. The soldiers are lined up one after another, stretching back into the mounds of dirt yet to be excavated. From a distance, they may appear identical. But a closer look shows each soldier has unique details to make him resemble a real person. Some have mustaches. Even their earlobes are different. Most of them are round, but approximately 20 percent are square— approximately the same ratio found in modern

A close examination of the warriors reveals the individuality present in their design and construction.

China. The soldier's age, the shape of his face, and his rank all seem to factor into the 25 different beard styles found on the warriors.[1]

Some bear the hint of a smile, but others are stern, the corners of their mouths turning downward. Some look fearful, others thoughtful, still others expectant, as if they look forward to the battle awaiting them. The looks in their eyes speak to the range of emotions displayed by these stone warriors. Their heights reflect their ranks, with officers being slightly taller than common soldiers. All are slightly taller than an average Chinese man of the time. Soldiers stand approximately six feet (1.8 m) tall, while generals are closer to six and one-half feet (2 m), heightening the impressive effect.[2]

Historians have debated where the sculptors found the inspiration to craft thousands of unique warriors. One possibility is the figures were modeled after actual soldiers in Qin's army. Another theory holds the artisans looked to people from their own lives, such as family members or neighbors, to design the warriors. In doing so, they could create figures that showed regional differences in the Chinese people, reflecting Qin's achievement of unifying the country under one ruler.

The realism of the terra-cotta warriors is matched by the detail of their horses.

In cavalry formations, powerful horses lined up four across, their hooves pounding across the battlefield, hurtling toward the enemy. The horses of the terra-cotta army recreate this magnificent scene. Flared nostrils and saddles sculpted to resemble leather enhance the realism. Decorations are woven into the horses' manes, while their tails are bound into knots to keep them from getting tangled in harnesses.

IN THE DETAILS

Prior to Qin, most Chinese art used a more decorative or evocative approach but was not particularly realistic. During Qin's time, people believed representations of people and objects could affect the deceased in their next life, so attention was given to details that would make them easily identifiable. The trick was to use the sculpture to recreate life, because in the afterlife the statues became the people they represented.

THE MAKING OF A SOLDIER

Although each soldier appears unique, closer inspection does reveal patterns. The artisans appear to have used molds to create some of the body parts, including heads and hands. This shortcut would have saved time. However, by attaching these parts in different combinations and at different angles, the sculptors achieved a wide variety of appearances. Ears and noses were shaped by hand and then attached, as were detailed ornaments on clothing, such as rivets or armor straps. Fine facial details, including hair, eyes, muscles, and wrinkles, were carved into a fine layer of clay smoothed over the larger figure.

Clay was an ideal medium. Other materials did not fit the bill for a variety of reasons. Bronze was too expensive for such large pieces. Wood decayed, and stone took too long to carve. Clay, however, was malleable, sturdy, cheap, and abundant. There was plenty of it in the ground around Mount Li.

Clay did pose some challenges, however. It had to be dense and sticky enough to stay together as the warrior was built and became heavier, but not too

TEMPERATURE SENSITIVITY

Clay statues are very sensitive to temperature. The best temperature at which to build them is approximately 68 degrees Fahrenheit (20°C). Unfortunately, Chinese summers are much hotter than this, and winters are much colder. In extreme temperatures, clay does not harden properly before it can be fired. Ancient artists may have solved the problem by using caves dug into the hillsides. Insulated by the earth, the caves would have maintained moderate temperatures, protecting the statues during the delicate construction phases. After the modeling was finished, the craftsmen may have sealed the entrance to the caves and turned them into kilns for firing.

Environmental conditions also pose a problem today. The vast size of the terra-cotta army, and the way the warriors are configured in their pits, makes it difficult to maintain specific levels of temperature and humidity that would optimally preserve the statues. Some scientists, worried that the statues are slowly decaying, suggest new ways of controlling airflow in order to better protect the warriors.

dense to dry out when it was fired in a kiln. To combat the problem of the statues becoming too heavy, the artisans built the warriors with solid legs to support their weight but left the upper bodies hollow. Each soldier had to be carefully balanced to avoid collapsing under his own weight or cracking during firing. Archaeologist Zhang Zhongli observes, "Whoever came up with the idea [of life-size soldiers] might not have known how difficult making them was going to be."[3]

THE GREEN WARRIOR

Most of the warriors in Qin's army were painted with pink skin. But one discovered in 1999 showed the remains of green paint. Archaeologists have proposed a number of theories for this anomaly. It might have been a joke, a mistake by a color-blind artist, or an effort to depict the darker skin of some soldiers. Another theory suggests this warrior was painted green to symbolize the bravery of the army, since in ancient China green represented youth and energy. The figure, a kneeling archer, could also have been a sniper whose face was painted green for camouflage. Snipers would have represented only a handful of the overall troops, which could help explain why only one green warrior was found.

Some parts of the statues retained much of their original paint.

61

Sculptors used a coiling technique to craft the bodies, winding strips of clay into coils and piling them upward in layers. Coiling takes longer than using molds. Artisans working today need approximately a month to replicate a terra-cotta soldier using the coiling process, whereas one sculpted with molds takes approximately half that time. But speed was not the point, notes Zhang. He says the sculptors purposely chose coiling to maximize the individuality of each statue. "Whether it was fat or slim, tall or short. . . . The idea was to create a group of humans."[4]

DRESSED FOR SUCCESS

The terra-cotta soldiers are now various shades of gray. However, archaeologists have uncovered tiny traces of paint on the statues. The remaining color offers clues to the warriors' original appearance.

The remaining paint on the warriors complicated the excavation project early on. As archaeologists brushed away the soil, the buried warriors were exposed to light and air for the first time in two millennia. Any traces of paint that remained began to flake and fade immediately.

The Chinese archaeology team, working with German conservators, scrambled to find out why. They discovered the statues had been originally covered with a layer of lacquer and then painted. When they were dug up, the water in the lacquer immediately evaporated, and the paint flaked off.

To combat the problem, archaeologists developed a method to treat the lacquer as soon as the statues were unearthed, preventing the water from evaporating and keeping the paint in place. From those small flecks of paint, archaeologists have been able to recreate the colors that were painted on the warriors in the first place: bright hues of green, red, white, blue, and a color known as Han purple. Catharina Blaensdorf, a German conservator who helped develop methods to treat the paint, says, "[They were] extremely colorful and each different. I did not find two with the same colors."[5]

The dress of the warriors also matches their rank. Generals, the most important people in the army, wear long coats with intricate designs of birds, suns, and abstract geometric patterns. Clay tassels on their shoulders and elaborate hats with pheasant feathers complete the uniform. Over their clothes are molded suits of armor, but the armor covers only their fronts, not their backs. This emphasizes their bravery, suggesting they would never retreat from battle.

ANCIENT PAINT

Most pigments and dyes in ancient China were manufactured from natural materials. But Han purple was a more complicated man-made color. It was only one of two artificial colors existing at the time, the other being Egyptian blue. Tests performed on tiny flecks of these paints confirm the two colors have similar ingredients. The difference is that Egyptian blue contains calcium while Han purple is made with barium and lead oxide. This suggests the knowledge to make artificial colors was developed independently in each country.

Soldiers from the infantry ranks have less elaborate clothing. Most are dressed in short pants and puttees, which are strips of cloth or leather wrapped around the lower part of the legs. Their shoes are wide and square. The sculptors did not ignore even the finest details here. One kneeling archer, poised on his toe for balance, shows the sole of his shoe. The sole exhibits wear on its tread, just as it would have in real life. Most of the infantry soldiers wear armor, but the archers at the front do not. Instead, they wear long robes fastened with a belt. This lighter clothing enabled them to move more quickly.

Hairstyles and headwear also reflect the warriors' ranks. Generals get the most elaborate hats, while lower officers have simpler caps. Most of the common soldiers are bareheaded, their long hair braided and wound into a topknot, usually positioned right of center.

CATHARINA BLAENSDORF

As a child, Catharina Blaensdorf liked to draw, paint, and work with her hands. But she did not want to be an artist. Instead, her interest in science led her to restoration work. Blaensdorf became an expert in the field of conservation at the Technical University in Munich, Germany.

Attracted to the idea of working on an international project, she began studying the paint on the terra-cotta warriors in the late 1990s. She soon discovered how fragile the paint can be. "Without conservation, the paint is completely lost [approximately] 1 week after excavation," she explains.[6] Working through a university in her native Germany, she helped develop and study new techniques to preserve the paint. Her work is making it possible to look into the colorful past of the terra-cotta army.

Researchers can learn a great deal from even tiny flakes of paint.

Ready for War

The terra-cotta soldiers' individuality of appearance stands in stark contrast to an army's purpose: to act as a cohesive unit, without hesitation or question. Rules and instructions governed each aspect of a soldier's job, from what he wore to how he stood. Who led the attack, who followed up, when they did it, where, and how—all was strictly regulated. This adherence to planning is visible in the terra-cotta army's formations and equipment.

Many of Qin's soldiers originally held weapons in their hands.

PROFESSIONAL WARFARE

In the centuries preceding Qin's rule, wars were conducted according to a strict code of conduct promoting chivalry. Rather than attack when it best suited them, both sides agreed to let their archers take turns firing at one another. If an enemy state was in mourning, fighting was suspended. During one battle in 632 BCE, the victorious army provided its conquered foes with three days of food. By the time of Qin's rule, however, war had become much more focused and professional. The idea was not to be nice but to win.

BATTLE FORMATION

Sun Zi, a Chinese military strategist who lived in the 400s BCE, changed the ways of war with his famous book *The Art of War*. The military principles he laid out in this book guided how military leaders conducted battles and managed their forces. Qin's highly organized armies are a stunning example of Sun Zi's strategies in action.

For example, Sun Zi wrote that the vanguard, or leading part of the army, must move quickly and flexibly and strike hard. In Qin's formations, the archery vanguard was positioned to rain a deadly shower of arrows on the enemy. They carried lighter equipment so they could move rapidly across the battlefield. The military units in Pit Two are arranged to maximize their flexibility. Rather than being lined up in parallel rows, they are grouped in a more modular formation. A perimeter line of standing archers surrounds a group of kneeling archers in one corner of the pit. Rows of chariots, sometimes interspersed with infantry soldiers or cavalry, are grouped in other areas of the pit. Together, the units were designed to work in a strategy called concentric deployment, meaning that each unit could function individually or as part of the larger whole.

During the Warring States period, the character of war changed. There were

BATTLE COMMUNICATION

Rather than war whoops, the crisp order of an officer, or the firing of a gun to announce battle, the ancient Chinese had their own method of communicating instructions to an army. Bells and drums have been found buried with the Qin warriors. The beating of a drum gave the order to advance, and the ringing of a bell signaled a regrouping of forces. People in charge of this function did their duty even when wounded.

more battles, and they lasted longer, demanding a steady supply of soldiers. Common men, rather than aristocrats, became the main battle force. Men were conscripted into the army for two years. In uneven terrain, foot soldiers could move more easily than chariots, and during Qin's rule, infantry soldiers formed the backbone of an army. Meanwhile, the use of cavalry was increasing, combining the speed and power of a chariot with the flexibility of a foot soldier.

Chariot warfare was in decline by Qin's time, as battles became more cutthroat, moving away from designated fields and instead being waged in rougher terrain. Still, these horse-drawn warriors were an integral part of battle. Chariots were comparable to today's tanks. The charioteer was flanked by two armed soldiers who would defend him.

THE WEAPONS OF THE WARRIORS

Ancient Qin warriors were armed for a variety of battle situations. They fought at close range with handheld weapons such as swords and spears. Some carried the versatile halberd, looking like a mix between an ax and a spear. Others used lances or short hooks. Longbows and powerful crossbows allowed archers to launch attacks from afar. Qin's terra-cotta warriors hold these same weapons—real, not clay—as they stand ready for battle.

Two unusual weapons found in the pits are the *pi* and the *Wu* hook. While descriptions of these weapons showed up in ancient records, archaeologists had never before found actual examples of them. The pi resembles a long lance. The blade is a little more than one foot (0.3 m) long, and it fits into a shaft approximately 12 feet (3.7 m) long.[1] It was ideal for a thrusting blow, and its length allowed the aggressor to keep a safe distance. The Wu hook was a lightweight but deadly weapon employing a two-foot (0.6 m) curved blade.[2]

In formation, Qin's archers took kneeling positions.

A staple in the arsenal of this ancient army was the bow. Hundreds of archers wielded both traditional longbows and more powerful crossbows. With a shooting range of approximately 2,600 feet (790 m), the crossbow was state-of-the-art weaponry.[3]

A few soldiers carried a *shu*, a long staff with a blunt, cylindrical bronze head approximately four inches (10 cm) long and resembling a drill bit.[4] Because this weapon has no blade, some historians believe it was simply a ceremonial weapon, but it might have had a functional use, too. Even a dull weapon could knock enemy cavalrymen off their horses or block an attack.

Most of the weapons are made from bronze, an alloy of metal containing copper and tin. Bronze was first made in China some 1,500 years before the Qin dynasty. While not as precious as gold or jade, bronze was still expensive. Its cost made it a luxury reserved for kings. Only the wealth of an imperial ruler would have been able to fund the construction of the thousands of bronze weapons found in the fists of the underground army.

The Qin metallurgists paid close attention to the quality of the weapons. They are carefully crafted to be of superior strength and quality. The tips of arrowheads, for example, are made from bronze containing a higher proportion of tin. Tin is a hard metal, and it is ideal for producing a sharp blade perfect for piercing the armor of an enemy soldier. Tin's strength has a drawback, though: it is brittle. So, the tangs of the arrows—the parts connecting the arrowhead to the shaft—have a lower tin content to make them more resilient.

Archaeologists found that even after being buried for 2,000 years, the blades on some of the warriors' swords remained sharp enough to finely cut through a hair or to devastate a leather shield. One archaeologist wrote, "Many of these pieces of military equipment are in such a pristine state of preservation that they would still be lethal today."[6] Even after centuries, they

IRON

While the technology to make iron emerged in China centuries before Qin's rule, it was not widely used for weapons. Bronze was more expensive than iron, but it was also stronger. In addition, iron manufacturing required a lot of time and work. Using it to mass-produce weapons was simply not practical. In one historical document dating from the 600s BCE, a Chinese ruler said, "The lovely metal [bronze] is used for casting swords and pikes. . . . The ugly metal [iron] is used for casting hoes which flatten weeds and axes which fell trees."[5] Very few iron weapons have been found in the Qin warrior pits, although the workers who built the pits did use iron tools such as hammers.

are still free of rust and look much as they did when they were first buried. Archaeologists discovered the weapons stood the test of time because they were treated with a protective coating made of chromium and salt. This technology was later discovered in Germany and the United States in the 1900s, but the ancient Chinese possessed it long before.

BRAVERY IN QIN'S ARMY

Qin's warriors were fiercely brave. Cowardice was not tolerated, and strict adherence to orders was expected. Any act of disobedience would have been swiftly taken care of by an officer—probably by chopping off the soldier's head. In *The Art of War*, Sun Zi gives one example of the strict Chinese discipline during the Warring States period. In his story, an enthusiastic soldier struck the enemy before the attack order had been issued. His attack was successful, and he presented his superiors with two heads of enemy soldiers. His reward was decapitation. His general commented, "I am confident he is an officer of ability, but he is disobedient."[7]

ARMOR

Armor became a military standard during the Warring States period. Small pieces of metal or leather were sewn onto a cloth backing. This armor was lightweight and allowed flexibility. It was not as sturdy or protective as a solid plate of armor, but it did provide some protection against sharp-edged weapons.

The armor worn by a warrior usually reflected his position and rank. An infantryman would be outfitted in armor with larger plates, but an officer's armor would be assembled from smaller plates packed more tightly together, allowing easier movement. Cavalrymen had shorter armor to let their legs move freely. The charioteers were obvious targets, unable to

The battle-worn versions of the armored helmets found in the pits would have offered Qin's infantrymen protection from sharp blades and arrows.

easily move from their position to dodge an enemy. Their armor was more protective, covering more of their lower bodies and extending down to their wrists to protect their vulnerable arms while they drove.

Shields were not widely employed in Qin's time. More things to carry would have meant slower progress. Historians believe the light outfitting of the soldiers indicates they were trained to attack rather than defend.

In a pit of armor excavated in 1998, researchers discovered tens of thousands of tiny limestone tiles. They were the remains of 150 suits of armor and 50 helmets.[8] They showed meticulous detail. Each was carefully crafted with rounded corners allowing it to mold comfortably to a human body. Tiny holes showed where thin bronze wires had tied the suits together. One set of armor used large diamond-shaped plates. Scholars have identified it as being part of a horse's set of armor. Before this find, archaeologists believed the earliest use of horse armor was several centuries later.

While the army's armor was highly faithful to real armor in its design, there is one major difference. The armor found in the pits was made of limestone, which would not have provided ample protection in real battle conditions. Thin and fragile, the limestone armor would have been shattered easily by a well-placed arrow. Instead, this armor was strictly for burial. Afterlife enemies

Archers in the army
wore relatively light
armor to permit them
to move quickly.

wield different weapons, and the
Chinese believed stone could
repel the evil forces found beyond
the grave.

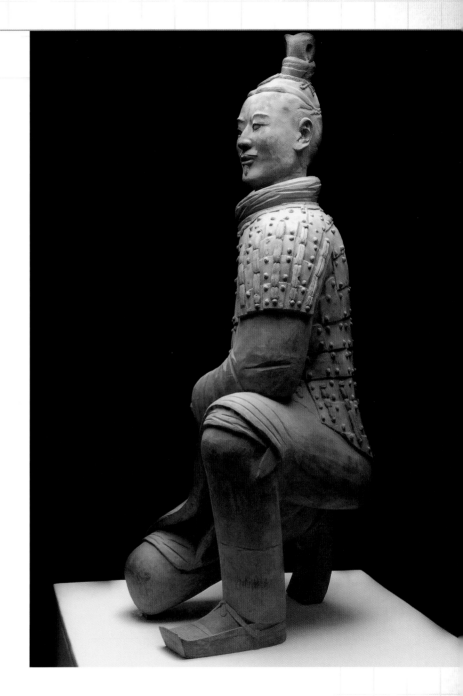

Acres of Treasures

Qin could afford everything life had to offer. Even in preparation for death, he had no intention of giving up the luxurious lifestyle to which he was accustomed. His mausoleum is an archaeologist's dream, a treasure trove filled with relics that are priceless not only because of their age and material value, but also for their ability to reconstruct a thriving society from 2,200 years ago.

Qin's army is so vast its museum was simply built around it.

A WHOLE CITY

With his army of warriors, Qin believed his safety was ensured in the afterlife. But since the discovery of the terra-cotta army, archaeologists have discovered the first emperor wanted more than just protection in the next world. He also wanted to enjoy the afterlife. To that end, he had many elements of his earthly existence recreated and buried with him.

Statues of musicians and acrobats stand by to provide the emperor with entertainment. These performers are crafted in more than a dozen poses representing a variety of activities, including displaying strength, spinning plates, juggling, and wrestling. The acrobats, excavated in 1999, also provide more evidence confirming Qin's far-reaching power. One researcher believes the poses of the acrobats indicate they came not from the Qin region in central China, but from farther south in present-day Myanmar.

If the emperor desired exercise, a pit was designed as the imperial stables. The bins in front of them still had scraps of the horses' feed. More than 30 smaller pits contained the skeletons of exotic birds and animals, which scholars believe represent the emperor's fondness for hunting.[1] In one pit, bronze swans, cranes, and geese were found next to a small stream. They are depicted in a variety of positions reflecting natural life. Some stand, while others rest. One is intently eating a worm.

However, not all of the civilian statues were for enjoyment. Some pits were constructed as government offices and are filled with civil officials provided with bamboo tablets for writing. The knives at their belts were used as erasers. Some historians believe these officials dealt with prisoners and judicial matters. These were important functions in Qin's dynasty.

In Qin's time, ancestors were always buried to the east of their descendants. To the west of the emperor's burial mound are smaller graves historians believe contain the bodies of his children and grandchildren. These people may have been killed by Qin's successor after he assumed the throne.

THE TOMB OF QIN

The entire complex surrounds one man: Qin himself. His burial mound is the centerpiece. From a distance, the tomb does not appear to be much at all. It is a hill, planted with trees, gently rising out of the lower fields. But underneath is where the legend lies.

CRANES

The cranes found in 2005 within Qin's mausoleum were put there as good omens. In China, the crane is considered a symbol of old age and wisdom. Cranes are believed to bring good luck and happiness. To tap into these benefits, pictures of cranes decorated the robes of high officials in ancient China. Members of the nobility kept live cranes as pets in their palaces, and paintings or statues of them accompanied the dead into the afterlife.

Sima Qian offered an amazing introduction to the tomb's contents. In his account he reports Qin's body was enclosed in a bronze coffin. The emperor was dressed for eternity in jade and gold and had pearls placed in his mouth. Around him, workers recreated a miniature version of China. They dug trenches to simulate rivers and filled them with liquid mercury. Pearls studded the copper-domed ceiling in starry constellations, a water clock kept the time, and lamps provided lighting.

No one would get in. Any trespassers would encounter strategically placed booby traps that would trigger a deadly crossbow. Furthermore, Sima Qian reports, after Qin was settled into his eternal home, the exits were sealed with the workers still inside so no one could escape and reveal its secrets.

No one knows for sure whether Sima Qian's report is true, because no modern archaeologists have been inside the tomb. Professor Wang Xueli of

DUTY CALLS

The people in Qin's court had one job: to serve the emperor. There is evidence that in Qin's mausoleum, real people, including concubines and servants, were buried with him. It is likely they did not follow him into death willingly, but this did not matter. Duty bound them to Qin, and they were forced to follow.

The mausoleum's location beneath a hill near the site of the warriors is known. Still, no archaeologists have yet excavated it.

the Shaanxi Provincial Archaeological Institute says simply, "It is the greatest enigma in archaeology."[2]

REMOTE SENSING

In 2002, the Chinese government launched a project using aerial photography and remote sensing techniques to survey Qin's burial site. Remote sensing is a noninvasive way of using high-tech methods to determine the presence of archaeological remains. For example, infrared scanners can register small differences in ground temperatures, which can point to buried buildings or artifacts. Archaeologists say it would have taken 200 years to survey the area using traditional methods. Using remote sensing technology, they have determined the location, boundaries, and depth of Qin's tomb in far less time.

MYTH OR REALITY?

There are tantalizing clues, however, that suggest at least part of this fantastic description has a factual basis. Scientists have probed the ground with sophisticated instruments to determine the overall size of the underground complex. Sunk 100 feet (30 m) into the ground, it has an overall area of approximately 820,000 square feet (76,000 sq m).[3] Two walls—an inner and an outer one—surround the tomb, simulating the layout of a palace. In 2007, using remote sensing technology, scientists found another pyramid-shaped room approximately 100 feet (30 m) high, built on top of Qin's actual burial site. The room's surrounding walls are constructed like ladders, suggesting that Qin's soul could climb them and travel into the afterlife.

Researchers have also detected the presence of mercury—the poisonous chemical rumored to flow in underground rivers—in amounts up to 100 times higher than normal levels.[4]

The mercury levels could provide evidence regarding the fate of the tomb. Some believe it still holds its precious treasures, while others think it was looted by rebel troops in the years after Qin's death. One archaeologist points out that if thieves had penetrated the tomb's depths, they would have released the mercury into the air and it would have evaporated. Instead, it still appears to be there.

Avoiding the toxic effects of mercury would be a problem for modern excavators too, even if their motives were simply academic. It is just one of many hurdles and controversies surrounding the issue of whether to excavate the tomb. There are other technical challenges in excavating such a large area, as well as challenges in preserving any artifacts once they surface. As archaeologists learned with the terra-cotta army, the ravages of time catch up quickly to artifacts once they are exposed to light and air.

Chinese archaeologists are divided about whether to proceed. Some advocate forging ahead; others are cautious and believe the tomb should be left alone until excavation technology is more advanced. Archaeologist Zhang Yinglan, who has worked with the warriors, said, "There is only one tomb of Qin Shihuangdi. We cannot afford to make any mistakes."[5] Another issue is more spiritual. In the Chinese culture, elders and ancestors are treated with great respect. Disturbing the dead is still a real concern. The attraction remains, however. Wang Xueli admits, "I don't dream about it at night. I dream about it during the day, when I am working."[6]

Though Qin's tomb remains undisturbed, work on the warriors continues at a cautious and deliberate pace.

A Lasting Legacy

Ancient artifacts are delicate things, subject to deterioration, breakage, and thievery. When excavation began on Qin's army and mausoleum, archaeologists knew protecting the warriors and other relics would be a challenge. The earth had shielded them up to this point, but now it was the archaeologists' turn to preserve the past.

Because the figures are in such close proximity to tourists, archaeologists must take extra precautions to preserve them.

PRESERVING THE FIGURES

Digging up some 8,000 figures is a monumental task. After nearly half a century, archaeologists are still only a quarter of the way through what they believe is the total size of the army. Figuring out where to actually put this army was an important dilemma the researchers faced. Due to the sheer size of the find, archaeologists elected not to move the soldiers to a museum, but rather to build a museum around them. The figures are displayed where they were originally found.

Pit One, the largest pit, was covered in 1976 with a large glass and concrete dome that protects the soldiers and allows in ample natural light for visitors and

Since the construction of the building over Pit One, most preservation work on the warriors has been carried out in a protected environment.

archaeologists. The architect in charge of the building, Li Naifu, remembers he faced a challenge when he was first charged with the project. He had to design something large enough to cover the soldiers, but inexpensive enough to be completed within his meager budget. Li remembers, "At that time, for that money, all we could think of was a simple arch. . . . So up it went, just like an enormous greenhouse."[1]

In 1989, a building went up over Pit Three, and in 1994, authorities built a larger one at Pit Two. The squat towers and black-tiled roofs were borrowed from the architectural styles of Qin's time. Today, the Qin Museum of the Terra-Cotta Warriors and Horses is huge, sprawling over a four-acre (1.6 ha) area.[2] Three more sites,

RECOGNITION

The Yang brothers received little fanfare for their monumental discovery. While the terra-cotta warriors have made the surrounding area prosperous through increased tourism, the brothers believe the Chinese government has largely ignored them. They have gotten little money or recognition as a result of the find. One brother complains official materials only say "local farmers" found the first warrior, rather than listing their names. But Zhao Kangmin, who reconstructed the first two soldiers, says he deserves even more credit than the farmers, because he was the one who recognized their historic and cultural value.

collectively known as the Lishan garden, are planned for the future. They will focus on the acrobats, civil officials, and stone armor found in nearby pits.

In addition to organizing all these statues and artifacts, scientists face another problem. In the mid-1990s, they found some 48 species of fungi growing in the warrior pits. One pit even had mushrooms sprouting up. Damp clay, bacteria carried in the breath of millions of visitors, and mild summer temperatures made it easy for the fungi to take hold. Scientists tackled the problem and have developed fungicides to destroy the intruders.

RECENT DISCOVERIES

In 2010, archaeologists began excavating the remains of a huge, ancient palace found within the mausoleum. With 18 courtyard buildings and a central main building, the site is approximately a quarter of the size of the famous Forbidden City in Beijing.[3] The palace shares one key attribute with the Forbidden City. Both are oriented along north-south axes, a position considered favorable according to ancient Chinese beliefs in cosmology. So far archaeologists have found walls and doorways for the buildings, as well as roads and the remains of a sewer system. It is the largest complex yet found on the grounds of Qin's mausoleum, and researchers hope it will reveal more information about the architecture of the emperor's times.

In the summer of 2012, archaeologists uncovered 110 more soldiers to add to Qin's army. They were found in a 2,152 square foot (200 sq m) pit along with 12 horses, the remains of chariots, and some weapons. Experts believe another 11 soldiers still lay underneath. This find was significant in that the soldiers were in remarkably good shape. Their paint had not deteriorated nearly as much as that on soldiers found in the three main pits.

THE FORBIDDEN CITY

Built in the 1400s during the Ming dynasty, Beijing's Forbidden City was the home of China's royalty for 500 years. Twenty-four emperors lived there during the Ming and Qing dynasties. Its design, featuring a symmetrical layout and many landscaped courtyards, is the classic model for Chinese palaces.

Together, the buildings of the Forbidden City contain approximately 10,000 rooms and cover an area of 8,000,000 square feet (740,000 sq m). Its name refers to the emperor's absolute power. It was forbidden for anyone to enter or leave the walled city without his permission.

In recent years, exhibitions of the terra-cotta soldiers have circled the globe, giving millions of people an up-close look at Qin's army.

A NEW IMAGE OF QIN

Much of what is known about Qin's life and reign comes from the writings of Sima Qian, the ancient historian who lived approximately a century after Qin. From him come the descriptions of Qin's lavish tomb and details about the style of Qin's rule. According to the historian, Qin was ruthless and unforgiving. He showed no mercy to those who crossed him or even simply questioned his decisions. But Sima Qian's depiction may be somewhat biased. Some scholars believe his characterizations may not have been aimed at Qin but rather at Wu, the emperor under whom Sima Qian lived. It could have been dangerous to criticize his own emperor, so Sima Qian may have sought to disguise his criticisms by assigning them to Qin. In addition, it was expected former dynasties should not be held in the same esteem as the reigning one. After all, the thinking went, if those dynasties had been decent and strong they would not have failed. The current rulers were expected to be treated as the best possible ones.

An associate who once visited with Qin reported afterward, "When in difficulties he willingly humbles himself, when successful he swallows men up without a scruple. . . . Should he succeed in conquering the [world], we shall all become his captives. There is no staying long with this man."[5] But documents found in 1975 revealed Qin's reputation as being vengeful and cruel may be exaggerated. Certainly, many of the punishments decreed by law were harsh, ranging from whipping to exile to imprisonment to execution. However, documents outlining the laws of the Qin dynasty suggest his legal code was also thorough and evenly applied.

Whatever shortcomings his administration had, the government was stable. While later dynasties changed aspects of it, its overall framework survived for centuries. "We find the underground pits are an imitation of the real organization in the Qin dynasty," says Duan Qingbo, an archaeologist who has worked on the project. "People thought when the emperor died, he took just a lot of pottery army soldiers with him. Now they realize he took a whole political system with him."[6]

The job of archaeology is to take scraps of information and piece them together into historical truth. According to some reports Qin was cruel, but according to others he was merely strict. Historians will debate Qin's legacy for years to come, but on one thing they agree: good or bad, Qin brought profound change to China. The legacy of his rule echoes through the centuries and into the present through his silent terra-cotta army.

A UNIQUE IDEA

The use of life-size figures for Qin's tomb seems to have been a one-time incident. There is no evidence of such statues from before or after him. However, the idea of constructing an army for the afterlife did live on. Terra-cotta armies guard several tombs dating from the Western Han dynasty, which immediately followed the Qin dynasty. However, the figures found in these are only approximately one-third life-size.[7]

Qin's army may not be able to physically protect him, but it guarantees his name will live on for millennia after his death.

TIMELINE

400s BCE

Sun Zi writes *The Art of War.*

475–221

China is in turmoil during the Warring States period.

259

Ying Zheng is born.

221

Zheng unites China after conquering all of the warring states and declares himself emperor, with the new title Qin Shihuangdi.

210

Qin dies suddenly, while on a trip around the country.

109

Sima Qian begins to write *Records of the Grand Historian*, which contains information about Qin and his rule.

1949 CE

Mao Zedong takes power in China.

1974

Farmers discover the first terra-cotta warrior in a village near Xi'an, China, and official excavation of the site begins several months later.

1987

Qin's mausoleum is named a UNESCO World Heritage Site.

1999

Statues of acrobats and performers are found in a satellite pit in the mausoleum complex.

2005

Bronze statues of cranes, swans, and geese are discovered in a pit designed to be a water garden.

2012

More than 100 additional soldiers and the ruins of a palace are found within the mausoleum complex.

DIGGING UP THE FACTS

DATE OF DISCOVERY

The warriors were discovered in 1974.

KEY PLAYERS

- Emperor Qin Shihuangdi ordered the construction of the terra-cotta army and mausoleum.

- The Yang brothers discovered the first terra-cotta warrior in 1974.

- Yuan Zhongyi led the excavation of the mausoleum.

KEY TECHNOLOGIES

Bronze was used to fashion the weapons held by the terra-cotta warriors. The artisans who built the warriors used special techniques, including assembly-line processes and temperature control. Remote-sensing technology gives archaeologists a look at delicate parts of the mausoleum that remain buried.

IMPACT ON SCIENCE

Each of the terra-cotta warriors is different, reflecting how China's different citizens were united under one rule, and demonstrating the skill the craftsmen possessed.

The arrangement of the warriors in the three main pits shows an army that was organized yet flexible, their formations and dress emphasizing offensive maneuvers. This gives clues to the military strategies of the time.

SEEING THE TERRA-COTTA ARMY

The best way to experience the full effect of the vast terra-cotta army is to visit the museum at the original excavation site, but some of the figures have also been sent on tour to museums around the world. For people unable to make the trip to China, these exhibitions are a great way to appreciate the stunning craftsmanship of the warriors. Only a few dozen figures at a time are permitted to leave the archaeological site, but the museum exhibits represent a unique opportunity to see one of the wonders of the world first-hand.

QUOTE

"There are seven wonders in the world, and we may say that the discovery of these terra-cotta warriors and horses is the eighth."—*Jacques Chirac*

GLOSSARY

alloy
A mixture of two or more metals.

black market
Trade in illegal goods.

cavalry
Soldiers who fight on horseback.

conscripted
Drafted into military forces.

dynasty
A line of related rulers of a country.

etymology
The origin and roots of a word.

hierarchical
Based on a system that assigns power and responsibility strictly according to rank.

infantry
Soldiers who fight on foot.

kiln
A large oven used for firing pottery.

malleable
Able to be pushed out of shape without cracking.

mausoleum
A large tomb.

nomadic
Roaming and not settled in one place.

terra-cotta
Clay fired at high temperatures to harden it.

vanguard
The advance portion of an army that would initiate an attack, supported by the main army.

ADDITIONAL RESOURCES

SELECTED BIBLIOGRAPHY

Roberto Ciarla, ed. *The Eternal Army: The Terracotta Soldiers of the First Chinese Emperor.* Vercelli, Italy: White Star, 2005. Print.

Shen, Chen. *The Warrior Emperor and China's Terracotta Army.* Toronto, ON: Royal Ontario Museum, 2010. Print.

Yuan, Zhongyi. *China's Terracotta Army and the First Emperor's Mausoleum.* Paramus, NJ: Homa & Sekey, 2011. Print.

FURTHER READINGS

Weimin, Xu. *Travel through the Middle Kingdom: Emperor Qin and his Terracotta Warriors.* New York: Better Link, 2006. Print.

Yang, Liu. *China's Terracotta Warriors: The First Emperor's Legacy.* Minneapolis, MN: Minneapolis Institute of Arts, 2012. Print.

WEBSITES

To learn more about Digging Up the Past, visit **booklinks.abdopublishing.com**. These links are routinely monitored and updated to provide the most current information available.

FOR MORE INFORMATION

For more information on this subject, contact or visit the following organizations:

THE MUSEUM OF QIN TERRA-COTTA WARRIORS AND HORSES

Qinling North Road

Lintong District

Xi'an 710600, China

86 29 8139 9001

The museum is the official repository of the terra-cotta warriors and offers visitors access to the mausoleum complex.

UNITED NATIONS EDUCATIONAL, SCIENTIFIC AND CULTURAL ORGANIZATION (UNESCO)

7, place de Fontenoy 75352

Paris 07 SP France

33 01 45 68 10 00

http://www.unesco.org

UNESCO works to promote communication between different countries, societies, and cultures. A UNESCO committee identifies properties all over the world that have outstanding cultural and natural value.

SOURCE NOTES

Chapter 1. A Silent Army

1. Chen Shen. *The Warrior Emperor and China's Terracotta Army*. Toronto, ON: Royal Ontario Museum, 2010. Print. 14.

2. Douglas Palmer. *Unearthing the Past*. Guilford, CT: Lyons, 2005. Print. 124.

3. Zhang Wenli. *The Qin Terracotta Army: Treasures of Lintong*. London: Scala, 1996. Print. 16.

4. Glenn Fieber. *Emperor of Stone*. Beijing, China: China Intercontinental, 2009. Print. 65.

5. John Man. *The Terra Cotta Army*. Cambridge, MA: Da Capo, 2008. Print. 224.

Chapter 2. The Discovery

1. Maxwell Hearn. "An Ancient Chinese Army Rises from Underground Sentinel Duty." *Smithsonian* Nov. 1979: 44. Print.

2. Frank Ching. "As China's Star Rises, So Too Does Fear." *China Post*. China Post, 14 Sept. 2011. Web. 5 June 2013.

3. Yu Fei. "Archaeologist Finds His Heaven." *China Daily*. China Daily, 13 Oct. 2009. Web. 3 Feb. 2014.

4. Ibid.

Chapter 3. The First Emperor

1. Arthur Cotterell. *The First Emperor of China.* New York: Holt, 1981. Print. 10.

2. Chen Shen. *The Warrior Emperor and China's Terracotta Army.* Toronto, ON: Royal Ontario Museum, 2010. Print. 40.

3. Ibid.

4. Maxwell Hearn. "An Ancient Chinese Army Rises from Underground Sentinel Duty." *Smithsonian* Nov. 1979: 39–40. Print.

5. "China's Terracotta Warriors: The First Emperor's Legacy." *China's Terracotta Warriors.* Minneapolis Institute of Arts, n.d. Web. 8 May 2013.

6. Arthur Cotterell. *The First Emperor of China.* New York: Holt, 1981. Print. 133.

Chapter 4. Glimpses into the Past

1. John Man. *The Terra Cotta Army.* Cambridge, MA: Da Capo, 2008. Print. 120.

2. Yuan Zhongyi. *China's Terracotta Army and the First Emperor's Mausoleum.* Paramus, NJ: Homa & Sekey, 2011. Print. 15.

3. Glenn Fieber. *Emperor of Stone.* Beijing, China: China Intercontinental, 2009. Print. 80.

4. Arthur Cotterell. *The First Emperor of China.* New York: Holt, 1981. Print. 22.

5. Zhang Wenli. *The Qin Terracotta Army: Treasures of Lintong.* London: Scala, 1996. Print. 82.

6. Roberto Ciarla, ed. *The Eternal Army: The Terracotta Soldiers of the First Chinese Emperor.* Vercelli, Italy: White Star, 2005. Print. 248.

7. Victoria Nesnick. "Secrets of the Tomb." *National Geographic World* Sept. 1999: 28. Print.

Chapter 5. The Figures in the Pits

1. Douglas Palmer. *Unearthing the Past.* Guilford, CT: Lyons, 2005. Print. 124.

2. Fu Tianchou. *Wonders from the Earth: The First Emperor's Underground Army.* San Francisco, CA: China Books and Periodicals, 1989. Print. 12, 14.

3. "China's Terracotta Warriors: Program Transcript." *Secrets of the Dead.* PBS, 5 May 2011. Web. 24 May 2013.

4. Ibid.

5. Ibid.

6. Matthew V. Veazey. "Old Warriors Get New Armor." *Materials Performance* Apr. 2004. 16–19. Print.

Chapter 6. Ready for War

1. Yuan Zhongyi. *China's Terracotta Army and the First Emperor's Mausoleum.* Paramus, NJ: Homa & Sekey, 2011. Print. 77.

2. Ibid. 74.

3. Glenn Fieber. *Emperor of Stone.* Beijing, China: China Intercontinental, 2009. Print. 112.

4. Zhang Tao. *China's First Emperor and his Terra-Cotta Army.* Shaanxi, China: Shaanxi Travel Tourism, 2005. Print. 77.

5. Yong Yap Cotterell and Arthur Cotterell. *The Early Civilization of China.* New York: Putnam, 1975. Print. 36.

6. Macros Martinón-Torres, et al. "Making Weapons for the Terracotta Army." *Archaeology International.* Institute of Archaeology, 22 Oct. 2011. Web. 31 May 2013.

7. Arthur Cotterell. *The First Emperor of China.* New York: Holt, 1981. Print. 44.

8. Roberto Ciarla, ed. *The Eternal Army: The Terracotta Soldiers of the First Chinese Emperor.* Vercelli, Italy: White Star, 2005. Print. 178.

Chapter 7. Acres of Treasures

1. Zhang Lin. *The Qin Dynasty Terra-Cotta Army of Dreams*. Xi'an, China: Xi'an Press, 2005. Print. 24.

2. "Emperor's Enigma: Tomb's Secrets Stay Sealed." *Washington Times*. Washington Times, 5 June 2003. Web. 24 May 2013.

3. Ibid.

4. Ibid.

5. Ibid.

6. Ibid.

Chapter 8. A Lasting Legacy

1. John Man. *The Terra Cotta Army*. Cambridge, MA: Da Capo, 2008. Print. 214.

2. Arthur Lubow. "Terra Cotta Soldiers on the March." *Smithsonian.com*. Smithsonian Institution, July 2009. Web. 5 May 2013.

3. Jonathan Kaiman. "China Unearths Ruined Palace Near Terracotta Army." *Guardian*. Guardian, 3 Dec. 2012. Web. 24 May 2013.

4. Chen Jia. "Ancient Warriors Never Get Old." *China Daily USA*. China Daily, 5 Apr. 2013. Web. 16 May 2013.

5. Frances Wood. *China's First Emperor and His Terracotta Warriors*. New York: St. Martin's, 2008. Print. 24–25.

6. Arthur Lubow. "Terra Cotta Soldiers on the March." *Smithsonian.com*. Smithsonian Institution, July 2009. Web. 5 May 2013.

7. Ann Paludan. *Chinese Sculpture: A Great Tradition*. Chicago, IL: Serindia, 2006. Print. 76.

INDEX

ABOUT THE AUTHOR

Diane Bailey has written 40 nonfiction books for teens on topics including sports, celebrities, government, finance, and technology. Her personal favorite is anything to do with history, whether ancient China, medieval Europe, or Civil War–era America. Diane also works as a freelance editor. She has two sons and two dogs, and she lives in Kansas.